READ & RESPOND

Bringing the best books to life in the classroom

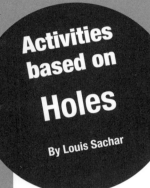

Activities based on
Holes
By Louis Sachar

Terms and conditions

IMPORTANT – PERMITTED USE AND WARNINGS – READ CAREFULLY BEFORE USING

IF YOU ACCEPT THE ABOVE CONDITIONS YOU MAY PROCEED TO USE THE CD-ROM.

Recommended system requirements:
Windows: XP (Service Pack 3), Vista (Service Pack 2), Windows 7 or Windows 8 with 2.33GHz processor
Mac: OS 10.6 to 10.8 with Intel Core™ Duo processor
1GB RAM (recommended)
1024 x 768 Screen resolution
CD-ROM drive (24x speed recommended)
Adobe Reader (version 9 recommended for Mac users)
Broadband internet connections (for installation and updates)

For all technical support queries (including no CD drive), please phone Scholastic Customer Services on 0845 6039091.

Designed using Adobe Indesign
Published by Scholastic Education, an imprint of Scholastic Ltd
Book End, Range Road, Witney, Oxfordshire, OX29 0YD
Registered office: Westfield Road, Southam,
Warwickshire CV47 0RA
www.scholastic.co.uk

Printed and bound by Ashford Colour Press
© 2016 Scholastic Ltd
2 3 4 5 6 7 8 9   7 8 9 0 1 2 3 4 5

British Library Cataloguing-in-Publication Data
A catalogue record for this book is available from the British Library.
ISBN 978-1407-14228-9

Extracts from *The National Curriculum in England, English Programme of Study* © Crown Copyright. Reproduced under the terms of the Open Government Licence (OGL). http://www.nationalarchives.gov.uk/doc/open-government-licence/version/3

Due to the nature of the web, we cannot guarantee the content or links of any site mentioned. We strongly recommend that teachers check websites before using them in the classroom.

Author Jillian Powell
Editorial team Rachel Morgan, Jenny Wilcox, Becky Breuer, Niamh O'Carroll, Jo Kemp, Elizabeth Evans
Series designer Neil Salt
Designer Anna Oliwa
Illustrator Judy Brown
Digital development Hannah Barnett, Phil Crothers and MWA Technologies Private Ltd

Acknowledgements
The publishers gratefully acknowledge permission to reproduce the following copyright material:

Bloomsbury Publishing Plc for the use of extracts and the cover from *Holes* by Louis Sachar. Text © 1998, Louis Sachar. (2000, Bloomsbury Publishing Plc).

Every effort has been made to trace copyright holders for the works reproduced in this book, and the publishers apologise for any inadvertent omissions.

CONTENTS

INTRODUCTION

Read & Respond provides teaching ideas related to a specific children's book. The series focuses on best-loved books and brings you ways to use them to engage your class and enthuse them about reading.

The book is divided into different sections:

- **About the book and author:** gives you some background information about the book and the author.

- **Guided reading:** breaks the book down into sections and gives notes for using it with guided reading groups. A bookmark has been provided on page 12 containing comprehension questions. The children can be directed to refer to these as they read.

- **Shared reading:** provides extracts from the children's books with associated notes for focused work. There is also one non-fiction extract that relates to the children's book.

- **Grammar, punctuation & spelling:** provides grammar, punctuation and spelling work related to the children's book so you can teach these skills in context.

- **Plot, character & setting:** contains activity ideas focused on the plot, characters and the setting of the story.

- **Talk about it:** has speaking and listening activities related to the children's book. These activities may be based directly on the children's book or be broadly based on the themes and concepts of the story.

- **Get writing:** provides writing activities related to the children's book. These activities may be based directly on the children's book or be broadly based on the themes and concepts of the story.

- **Assessment:** contains short activities that will help you assess whether the children have understood concepts and curriculum objectives. They are designed to be informal activities to feed into your planning.

The activities follow the same format:

- **Objective:** the objective for the lesson. It will be based upon a curriculum objective, but will often be more specific to the focus being covered.

- **What you need:** a list of resources you need to teach the lesson, including digital resources (printable pages, interactive activities and media resources, see page 5).

- **What to do:** the activity notes.

- **Differentiation:** this is provided where specific and useful differentiation advice can be given to support and/or extend the learning in the activity. Differentiation by providing additional adult support has not been included as this will be at a teacher's discretion based upon specific children's needs and ability, as well as the availability of support.

The activities are numbered for reference within each section and should move through the text sequentially – so you can use the lesson while you are reading the book. Once you have read the book, most of the activities can be used in any order you wish.

Below are brief guidance notes for using the CD-ROM. For more detailed information, please click on the '?' button in the top right-hand corner of the screen.

The program contains the following:

- the extract pages from the book
- all of the photocopiable pages from the book
- additional printable pages
- interactive on-screen activities
- media resources.

Getting started

Put the CD-ROM into your CD-ROM drive. If you do not have a CD-ROM drive, phone Scholastic Customer Services on 0845 6039091.

- For Windows users, the install wizard should autorun, if it fails to do so then navigate to your CD-ROM drive. Then follow the installation process.
- For Mac users, copy the disk image file to your hard drive. After it has finished copying double click it to mount the disk image. Navigate to the mounted disk image and run the installer. After installation the disk image can be unmounted and the DMG can be deleted from the hard drive.
- To install on a network, see the ReadMe file located on the CD-ROM (navigate to your drive).

To complete the installation of the program you need to open the program and click 'Update' in the pop-up. Please note – this CD-ROM is web-enabled and the content will be downloaded from the internet to your hard drive to populate the CD-ROM with the relevant resources. This only needs to be done on first use, after this you will be able to use the CD-ROM without an internet connection. If at any point any content is updated, you will receive another pop-up upon start up when there is an internet connection.

Main menu

The main menu is the first screen that appears. Here you can access: terms and conditions, registration links, how to use the CD-ROM and credits. To access a specific book click on the relevant button (NB only titles installed will be available). You can filter by the

drop-down lists if you wish. You can search all resources by clicking 'Search' in the bottom left-hand corner. You can also log in and access favourites that you have bookmarked.

Resources

By clicking on a book on the Main menu, you are taken to the resources for that title. The resources are: Media, Interactives, Extracts and Printables. Select the category and then launch a resource by clicking the play button.

Teacher settings

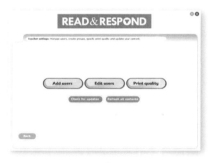

In the top right-hand corner of the screen is a small 'T' icon. This is the teacher settings area. It is password protected, the password is: login. This area will allow you to choose the print quality settings for interactive activities ('Default' or 'Best') and also allow you to check for updates to the program or re-download all content to the disk via Refresh all content. You can also set up user logins so that you can save and access favourites. Once a user is set up, they can enter by clicking the login link underneath the 'T' and '?' buttons.

Search

You can access an all resources search by clicking the search button on the bottom left of the Main menu. You can search for activities by type (using the drop-down filter) or by keyword by typing into the box. You can then assign resources to your favourites area or launch them directly from the search area.

CURRICULUM LINKS

Section	Activity	Curriculum objectives
Guided reading		Comprehension: To discuss their understanding of what they have read. Comprehension: To draw inferences and justify inferences with evidence. Comprehension: To summarise the main ideas, identifying key details that support the main ideas.
Shared reading	1	Comprehension: To draw inferences such as inferring characters' feelings. Composition: To use synonyms.
	2	Comprehension: To draw inferences such as inferring characters' feelings. To discuss and evaluate how authors use figurative language.
	3	Comprehension: To draw inferences, justifying inferences with evidence. Transcription: To investigate spellings and understand that some words need to be learned specifically.
	4	Comprehension: To discuss and evaluate how authors use figurative language. Comprehension: To retrieve information from non-fiction.
Grammar, punctuation & spelling	1	Composition: To use passive verbs.
	2	Composition: To use synonyms and antonyms.
	3	Transcription: To distinguish between and use homophones and other words which are often confused.
	4	Composition: To use relative clauses. Composition: To use commas to clarify meaning.
	5	Composition: To use the passive voice. Composition: To use synonyms and antonyms. Transcription: To use a thesaurus.
	6	Transcription: To understand that some words need to be learned specifically. Transcription: To use a dictionary.
Plot, character & setting	1	Composition: To describe settings, characters and atmosphere.
	2	Composition: To describe settings, characters and atmosphere.
	3	Comprehension: To ask questions to improve understanding. Composition: To describe settings, characters and atmosphere.
	4	Composition: To select the appropriate form for the purpose of the writing.
	5	Comprehension: To draw inferences, justifying inferences with evidence. Comprehension: To ask questions to improve understanding.
	6	Comprehension: To draw inferences, justifying inferences with evidence. Comprehension: To predict what might happen from details stated and implied.
	7	Comprehension: To ask questions to improve understanding. Comprehension: To identify how structure contributes to meaning. To make comparisons within books.
	8	Comprehension: To identify how language, structure and presentation contribute to meaning. Comprehension: To learn technical terms such as simile, imagery, style and effect.

Section	Activity	Curriculum objectives
Talk about it	1	Spoken language: To give well-structured descriptions, explanations and narratives.
	2	Comprehension: To draw inferences, justifying them with evidence. Spoken language: To participate in performances, role play, improvisations and debates.
	3	Comprehension: To draw inferences, such as inferring characters' feelings. Spoken language: To participate in performances, role play, improvisations and debates. Spoken language: To use spoken language to develop understanding through imagining and exploring ideas.
	4	Spoken language: To consider and evaluate different viewpoints, attending to and building on the contributions of others.
	5	Comprehension: To identify and discuss themes. Spoken language: To gain, maintain and monitor the interest of the listener(s). Spoken language: To select and use appropriate registers for effective communication.
	6	Comprehension: To draw inferences, such as inferring characters' feelings. Spoken language: To participate in performances, role play and improvisations.
Get writing	1	Composition: To ask questions to improve understanding. To assess the effectiveness of their own and others' writing and suggest improvements.
	2	Composition: To identify the audience and purpose of writing and select the appropriate form.
	3	Composition: To select the appropriate form for the purpose of the writing. Comprehension: To infer characters' feelings. Composition: To distinguish between informal and formal language.
	4	Composition: To identify the audience and purpose of writing and select appropriate form.
	5	Comprehension: To discuss themes in the novel. Composition: To organise paragraphs around a theme.
	6	Composition: To use organisational and presentational features to structure text. Comprehension: To distinguish between statements of fact and opinion.
Assessment	1	Composition: To précis longer passages. Comprehension: To summarise the main ideas from more than one paragraph.
	2	Comprehension: To identify and discuss themes.
	3	Comprehension: To explain and discuss their understanding of what they have read. Comprehension: To provide reasoned justifications for their views.
	4	Comprehension: To recognise and compare themes in what they read.
	5	Comprehension: To explain and discuss their understanding of what they have read. Comprehension: To provide reasoned justifications for their views.
	6	Comprehension: To explain and discuss their understanding of what they have read. Comprehension: To provide reasoned justifications for their views.

▼ HOLES

About the book

The novel *Holes* resembles one of the onions that feature prominently in the story as the magical cure-all vegetable sold by the young black onion grower, Onion Sam. As the plot unfolds, it reveals layers of stories, beginning with a young Stanley Yelnats IV being sent to Camp Green Lake, a juvenile correction facility, on a false charge for a crime he did not commit. Set in a desert wasteland of Texas, the plot lines evolve and interweave; Stanley's own story is set in the context of his family history, beginning with his great-great-grandfather Elya Yelnats, whose broken promise invokes a gypsy curse (so the family believes) on his descendants, including Stanley.

The author, Louis Sachar, has said that all of his other novels began with the idea for a 'piece of a character', but *Holes* began with a sense of place, Camp Green Lake, inspired by the brutal heat of the summers in Texas where he lives. The plot and characters grew out of this harsh desert terrain, as the author developed a detective mystery, intertwined with themes of redemption, growing up and friendship. Along the way, Stanley grows from a shy boy lacking in confidence and bullied at school into a courageous survivor, learning values like patience, tolerance and loyalty as the tightly constructed plot weaves its way towards resolution. This places the book in the tradition of American 'coming of age' novels such as JD Salinger's *The Catcher in the Rye* (1951) and Harper Lee's *To Kill a Mockingbird* (1960). Sachar describes Stanley as a 'pathetic kid', who lifts himself to heroic status by the selfless act of carrying his new-found friend Zero up the mountain and saving his life, a redemptive act that rights the wrong his great-great-grandfather committed. Originally titled '*Wrong Place, Wrong time, Wrong Kid*', *Holes* took eighteen months and five drafts to compose, and has since inspired two companion novels: *Stanley Yelnats' Survival Guide to Camp Green Lake* (2003) and *Small Steps* (2006).

About the author

Louis Sachar was born in New York in 1954. When he was nine, the family moved to California, where at high school he discovered his love of reading. He went on to college in Ohio, then California to study economics, and found work as a teacher's assistant in a primary school. After he graduated in 1976, he wrote the first of his *Wayside School* stories, based on the Hillside Elementary School where he was working. He then pursued a legal career, studying at law college in San Francisco and doing part-time legal work while writing for children in the evenings. From 1989, he became a full-time children's author, becoming widely known through the novel *Holes*. He lives in Austin, Texas, writing every morning for two hours, and enjoying games of bridge with friends. He has had over 21 books published, including the *Marvin Redpost* and *Wayside School* series.

Key facts

Holes
Author: Louis Sachar
First published: 1998, in America, by Farrar, Straus & Giroux Inc
Awards: Winner of the National Book Award 1998, New York Times best book of the year, winner of The Newbery Medal 1999.
Did you know? *Holes* was adapted into a Disney film 2003.

First look

Look together at the cover of *Holes*. Ask the children what sort of story they think this will be. (An adventure, mystery, thriller, detective story?) Ask: *What do the scrubby terrain and the lizard, with its piercing red eye, convey?* (The story is set in a desert, which is inhabited by sinister or dangerous reptiles.) Next read the back cover blurb. Pick out the words 'miscarriage of justice' and check that the children understand the meaning – that a boy called Stanley has been wrongly accused or sentenced for a crime he did not commit. Ask: *What is a juvenile detention centre?* (A place where young people are sent to spend time when they have committed a crime, to punish them and improve their behaviour.) *What kind of place do you think Camp Green Lake might be?* (Encourage a variety of views here.) *What is the main hook or mystery in the blurb that makes the reader want to read the story?* (To find out the true reason why the Warden wants the boys to dig holes in the lake bed.) Ask the children to extract key words from the reviews that tell us more about the type of story (simply written prose and 'funny'; 'tightly plotted detective novel' with 'plot twists'; themes of 'friendship'). Ask: *What do they tell us about its style, plot and themes?*

Chapters 1–4

Turn to the title page of Part One and read the heading. Ask: *What does it remind us of?* (a road sign, telling drivers their location – tell the children these are frequently used in America) Read Chapter 1 together and ask the children what kind of place the camp sounds like. (harsh, bleak, dangerous) Ask: *How would you describe the writing style?* (simple, matter-of-fact, informal) Highlight the use of single-word sentences: 'Usually.' 'Always.' Ask what impact these have. (They are casual, matter-of-fact asides about deadly dangers.) Highlight question 12 on the Guided Reading bookmark.

Continue reading to the end of Chapter 4. Ask the children to précis the main facts they have learned. (Stanley is going to Camp Green Lake for 18 months after being arrested; his great-grandfather Stanley Yelnats was robbed by a famous outlaw.) *What key information is left unexplained?* (why Stanley was arrested) *What can we infer about where the story is set, and how?* (It is set in America, which we can deduce from the reference to Texas and American English words/spellings such as 'cot' meaning bed, and 'counselor'.) Refer to question 10 on the Guided Reading bookmark.

Chapters 5–6

Read the next two chapters. Can the children explain why Stanley was sent to Camp Green Lake? (He was arrested for stealing a pair of sneakers belonging to a famous baseball player.) Ask: *Why is it worse for him that he tells the truth about what happened?* (They fell from the sky, which sounds incredible.) *What does Stanley attribute his misfortune to?* (A curse on his family by a one-legged gypsy whom his great-great-grandfather had wronged by stealing a pig, many years earlier.)

Chapter 7

Read on to the end of Chapter 7. Pause and highlight the flashback to Elya's story. Ask: *What is the significance of this in Stanley's life?* (It invokes the curse on his family, so they believe.) *Why do you think Elya gave up on Myra?* (She hesitates instead of returning his love, and leaves her choice up to chance.) *What promise does Elya fail to keep?* (To carry Madame Zeroni up the mountain.) Elicit how the present and past plots are interwoven, and tell the children to listen out for the flashbacks as the novel progresses, asking volunteers to raise their hand whenever they hear a flashback. Focus on question 9 on the Guided Reading bookmark.

Chapters 8–9

Read the next two chapters; then ask: *What shows that the other boys have accepted Stanley as one of the gang?* (They have given him the nickname 'Caveman'.) Refer to question 3 on the Guided Reading bookmark. Ask: *What does Stanley think is strange about them and what do they think is strange about Stanley?* (They have wrecked their own recreation room; he is writing a letter to his mother.)

Chapters 10–15

Continue reading to the end of Chapter 15. Ask the children what hook or mystery drives the plot forward in this part of the novel. (Why is the Warden really making the boys dig holes every day? What is it she is searching for?) Ask: *What secret advantage does Stanley now hold even though X-ray took the credit for finding the gold tube?* (He knows where it was really found, and that the boys are now digging in the wrong place.) At the end of Chapter 12 pause to discuss question 16 on the Guided Reading bookmark.

Ask the children how they think they would cope with life at the camp. Discuss question 15 on the Guided Reading bookmark.

Chapters 16–17

Read the next two chapters and pause to reflect on what we learn about the Warden's and Zigzag's characters. (They can both be cruel or even dangerous.)

Chapters 18–22

Read on to the end of Chapter 22. Ask the children to explain the repercussions of the sunflower seed incident and how it moves the plot on. (Stanley takes the blame although he is innocent; Zero then digs his hole for him, and Stanley agrees to teach him in return for the help with digging; the Warden is again revealed as a sinister, dangerous character; and Stanley finally realises the significance of the gold tube.)

Chapters 23–25

Read to the end of Chapter 25, checking that the children register the flashbacks from present to past. Ask: *What has made Stanley's life at camp a bit better?* (his deal with Zero) *What has made it worse?* (Mr Sir now bears a grudge and is punishing him.) Ask them to précis what we learn about Katherine Barlow and Sam, and cite evidence for racism in Green Lake. (Sam was not allowed to attend school as he is a Negro; Hattie Parker is outraged when she sees Sam kissing a white woman.)

Chapters 26–28

Read to the end of Part One, and ask the children to summarise the plot, and why Green Lake has suffered the curse of drought (possible inference that this is God's punishment for the racist murder of Sam and the people's cruelty to Sam and Kate because of their racial prejudices). Together, discuss questions 11 and 14 on the Guided Reading bookmark.

Chapters 29–34

Read from the beginning of Part Two to the end of Chapter 34, pausing to ask the children to highlight clues in Chapter 29 that something is about to happen: the brewing storm and the lightning over the rock suggest that something is afoot. Ask: *How does Stanley's life now echo that of his great-grandfather?* (He is wandering the desert, trying to survive and looking for water.) Check that they understand the link with the past as he finds Sam's boat, which sank on the lake when Sam was shot by Trout Walker.

Chapters 35–44

Continue reading, pausing to ask the children to explain echoes or links with the past: the spiced peaches, which Kate had carried on the boat; the rock where Stanley's great-grandfather had found refuge. Ask: *When Stanley carries Zero up the mountain, whose unfulfilled promise does this echo and fulfil?* (That of Elya, his great-great-grandfather, who failed to honour his promise to carry Madame Zeroni up the mountain.) Ask the children to discuss question 5 on the Guided Reading bookmark.

Chapters 45–49

Continue reading to the end of Chapter 48. Together, discuss question 2 on the bookmark. Pause to ask the children to highlight the questions that are finally answered: the Warden had been searching for the suitcase, containing the loot stolen from Stanley's great-grandfather by the outlaw Kate Barlow, and Zero had taken the sneakers belonging to Clyde Livingston. Focus on question 6 on the bookmark.

Ask: *Why do you think that rain begins to fall on Green Lake again?* (Wrongs have been righted and the curse lifted.) Review question 4 on the Guided Reading bookmark.

Chapter 50

Read on to the end of the novel. Together, focus on questions 7 and 8 on the Guided Reading bookmark. Ask: *Who is the woman who fluffs Hector's hair?* (his mother, found with the help of a private investigator) Ask the children to list other things that have come 'right'. (Stanley's father has invented his foot-odour product, now endorsed by Clyde Livingston; the camp has been closed; the Walker land has become a Girl Scout camp – check that they understand the irony of this, given Mr Sir's constant refrain, "This isn't a Girl Scout camp.")

Ask the children their views on the ending: *How do things work out overall for Stanley?* Discuss questions 1 and 13 on the bookmark. Ask: *Is the ending satisfactory and heart-warming or it a bit too perfect, neatly tidying all the loose ends or 'filling in all the holes', to use the author's metaphor?* Encourage a range of subjective opinions.

■ SCHOLASTIC
READ & RESPOND
Bringing the best books to life in the classroom

Holes
by Louis Sachar

Focus on...
Meaning

1. How is Camp Green Lake supposed to build character? Why and how does it change Stanley?

2. How long is Stanley at Camp Green Lake? Skim and scan to work it out.

3. Name two ways the other boys show Stanley they have accepted him.

4. What links Stanley to Zero (a) in the past, and (b) in the theft of the sneakers?

5. How long are Stanley and Zero 'on the run'? Find clues.

6. What evidence proves that Stanley was wrongly accused?

7. Who ruffles Zero's hair at the end? How are other problems resolved?

Focus on...
Organisation

8. Why is the book in three parts? What are the shifts in plot that divide them?

9. The book moves between the distant past, recent past and present. What links them?

■ SCHOLASTIC
READ & RESPOND
Bringing the best books to life in the classroom

Holes
by Louis Sachar

Focus on...
Language and features

10. Note any examples you find of American English terms; for instance, cookie, cot, sneakers.

11. How does the author create contrast between Camp Green Lake in the past and in the present? List some words and phrases describing each landscape.

12. Find examples of informal speech or dialogue, where grammar or sentence structure is incorrect.

Focus on...
Purpose, viewpoints and effects

13. Is Stanley a hero or an anti-hero? Give reasons why.

14. How do superstition and ideas of destiny feature in the plot?

15. How do you think you would cope with life at Camp Green Lake? What would you find hardest and why?

16. Stanley is wrongly accused. How does he react to this and why? What does this show us about his character?

Extract 1

- Read an enlarged copy of Extract 1. Ask the children how Stanley is feeling (weary, bored, resigned). Ask: *What is it that glistens in the soil?* (The lipstick case once owned by Kate Barlow.)

- Ask them how the author uses repetition to emphasise the monotony of Stanley's task. Underline the sentence *He dug his shovel into the dirt*, which is repeated four times.

- Ask: *Which sentences are incomplete grammatically?* Circle or underline the third, fourth and fifth sentences, which all lack a subject. Ask: *What effect do these short, incomplete sentences have?* (They emphasise the tedium and regularity of the task, and speed up the pace as they are summarising action or events over days and weeks.)

- Challenge the children to find all the words that describe the act of digging: *sticking*, *dug* (repeated), *dig*. Ask: *What verbs could replace them?*

- Ask them to find three examples of American English ('figured', 'gotten', 'canteen'). Ask: *What are some British English words that could be used instead?* (guessed/thought, become/got, flask)

- Ask the children why this is a significant moment in the plot. (It begins the chain of events that ends with Stanley's release and the discovery of the suitcase owned by the first Stanley Yelnats.) Ask: *What clues or signs are there that suggest change is on the way?* (A cloud has appeared, a sign of the rain that will fall once again on the lake when Stanley has righted a past wrong and natural order has been restored.)

Extract 2

- Read an enlarged copy of Extract 2. Ask the children to infer the feelings of each character described (Katherine and Sam's love for each other, Hattie Parker's racism and contempt).

- Ask what we can infer from each of the following:
  - 'The only person who wasn't happy with it was Miss Katherine. She'd run out of things needing to be fixed.' (She was using the jobs around the school as an excuse to see more of Sam.)
  - 'No water leaked into the classroom, except for the few drops that came from her eyes.' (She is crying and unhappy that she no longer sees Sam every day.)
  - '"I can fix that," said Sam.' (He has fixed the schoolhouse and now he can fix her breaking heart, through love.)

- Ask: *What does the adjective 'quivering' suggest?* (Hattie Parker is angered at what she sees.) Point out that sometimes the author implies or suggests rather than explicitly states, inviting the reader to draw inferences.

- Challenge the children to find an example of a metaphor ('freshly painted jewel') and onomatopoeia ('pitter-patter').

- Circle 'Onion Sam' and ask the children to explain the nickname. (Sam grows and sells onions, which he believes have healing powers.) Underline or circle the word 'semester' and ask children to replace it with a British English equivalent (school term).

- Underline Hattie Parker's words and ask the children to explain her prejudice and whether her threat is valid. Ask: *Who really gets punished – how and why?* (The community at Green Lake when the drought sets in, because of the racist killing.)

Extract 3

- Read an enlarged copy of Extract 3. Ask the children to explain what Stanley is trying to do and why (reach the rock called God's Thumb, where his great-grandfather found refuge, and where he hopes to find water so he and Zero can survive).

- Ask the children to concentrate on all the strong, active verbs that suggest 'effort' and circle them. ('took', 'pulled', 'stooped', 'lifting', 'climbed'). Ask the children to find a short sentence that emphasises Stanley's struggle by means of the word order and also repetition. ('Higher and higher he climbed.')

- Circle the words 'foul odor' and ask the children to replace the American English with the British English spelling of the noun (odour). Ask: *Where is the odour coming from?* (The boys are crossing Sam's onion field.)

- Ask: *What does the growth of the onion plants suggest?* (That there is water nearby.)

- + the children find a simile and a metaphor? ('like a giant magnet'; 'the bitter smell of despair')

- Challenge the children to explain how this passage interweaves plots from the past and the present. (Stanley is carrying Madame Zeroni's great-great-great-grandson up the mountain, righting the wrong Elya Yelnats did when he failed to carry her up the mountain as he promised, and so lifting the Yelnats' family curse; they have found Sam's onion field, and the onions help them survive and so stop Trout Walker's granddaughter, the Warden, finding the loot Katherine Barlow – or Kissin' Kate – stole from Stanley's great-grandfather.)

Extract 4

- Read an enlarged copy of Extract 4. Ask the children who they think the text is aimed at. (tourists or visitors to the desert, probably from the United States as certain words/spellings suggest) Ask: *What kind of impression of the desert does it give?* (spectacular terrain, interesting plant and wildlife, challenging activities)

- Ask children to identify adjectives that help to create a visual picture of the landscape. ('bleak', 'intimidating', 'endless', 'monotonous', 'towering', 'unrelenting', 'scorching')

- Ask them to find a simile. ('like scenes in a Western movie') Focus on the imagery used and circle metaphorical verbs ('shrouded', 'punctuated', 'bristles', 'cruising') and phrases ('diamond-hard'; 'photographer's and painter's paradise'). Discuss the resonances created by each metaphor ('shrouded': a flimsy white covering like a shroud, 'punctuated': dotted here and there; 'bristles': covered with spikes and spines; 'cruising': moving slowly and smoothly as if sailing on water; 'diamond-hard': light that is sparkling and clear like a diamond; 'paradise': a perfect place for painters and photographers).

- Ask: *What examples of alliteration can you find?* (for example, 'graceful golden', 'cruising currents')

- Ask the children to suggest any words they could replace with British English spelling or forms. ('highways' = motorways; 'canteen' = flask; 'sun shades' = sunglasses; 'color' = colour)

- Challenge the children to find any elements of the description that are echoed in the novel (the scorching heat, the harshness of the landscape, the dried-up lake, the venomous snakes and lizards). Underline words that suggest the bleak or harsh nature of the desert ('bleak', 'intimidating', 'tough', 'survive', 'scorching').

Extract 1

Chapter 13

All too soon Stanley was back out on the lake, sticking his shovel into the dirt. X-Ray was right: the third hole was the hardest. So was the fourth hole. And the fifth hole. And the sixth, and the…

He dug his shovel into the dirt.

After a while he'd lost track of the day of the week, and how many holes he'd dug. It all seemed like one big hole, and it would take a year and a half to dig it. He guessed he'd lost at least five pounds. He figured that in a year and a half he'd be either in great physical condition, or else dead.

He dug his shovel into the dirt.

It couldn't always be this hot, he thought. Surely it got cooler in December. Maybe then they froze.

He dug his shovel into the dirt.

His skin had gotten tougher. It didn't hurt so much to hold the shovel.

As he drank from his canteen he looked up at the sky. A cloud had appeared earlier in the day. It was the first cloud he could remember seeing since coming to Camp Green Lake.

He and the other boys had been watching it all day, hoping it would move in front of the sun. Occasionally it got close, but it was just teasing them.

His hole was waist deep. He dug his shovel into the dirt. As he dumped it out, he thought he saw something glisten as it fell onto the dirt pile. Whatever it was, it was quickly buried.

Extract 2

Chapter 25

By the end of the first semester, Onion Sam had turned the old, run-down schoolhouse into a well-crafted, freshly painted jewel of a building that the whole town was proud of. People passing by would stop and admire it. "That's our schoolhouse. It shows how much we value education here in Green Lake."

The only person who wasn't happy with it was Miss Katherine. She'd run out of things needing to be fixed.

She sat at her desk one afternoon, listening to the pitter-patter of the rain on the roof. No water leaked into the classroom, except for the few drops that came from her eyes.

"Onions! Hot sweet onions!" Sam called, out on the street.

She ran to him. She wanted to throw her arms around him but couldn't bring herself to do it. Instead she hugged Mary Lou's neck.

"Is something wrong?" he asked her.

"Oh, Sam," she said. "My heart is breaking."

"I can fix that," said Sam.

She turned to him.

He took hold of both her hands, and kissed her.

Because of the rain, there was nobody else out on the street. Even if there was, Katherine and Sam wouldn't have noticed. They were lost in their own world.

At that moment, however, Hattie Parker stepped out of the general store. They didn't see her, but she saw them. She pointed her quivering finger in their direction and whispered, "God will punish you!"

Extract 3

Chapter 38

Stanley took hold of Zero's forearms and pulled him upright. Then he stooped down and let Zero fall over his right shoulder. He stood up, lifting Zero's worn-out body off the ground.

He left the shovel and sack of jars behind as he continued up the mountain. Zero's legs dangled in front of him.

Stanley couldn't see his feet, which made it difficult to walk through the tangled patches of weeds and vines. He concentrated on one step at a time, carefully raising and setting down each foot. He thought only about each step, and not the impossible task that lay before him.

Higher and higher he climbed. His strength came from somewhere deep inside himself and also seemed to come from the outside as well. After focusing on Big Thumb for so long, it was as if the rock had absorbed his energy and now acted like a kind of giant magnet pulling him toward it.

After a while, he became aware of a foul odor. At first, he thought it came from Zero, but it seemed to be in the air, hanging heavy all around him.

He also noticed that the ground wasn't as steep anymore. As the ground flattened, a huge stone precipice rose up ahead of him, just barely visible in the moonlight. It seemed to grow bigger with each step he took.

It no longer resembled a thumb.

And he knew he'd never be able to climb it.

Around him, the smell became stronger. It was the bitter smell of despair.

Extract 4

Explore the Chihuahuan!

To the uninitiated, the desert can appear a bleak and intimidating place, reached by endless, monotonous highways that seem to stretch into infinity. But the landscapes of the Chihuahuan, which reaches from western Texas across southern New Mexico and into Arizona, generously unfold their treasures to the more adventurous traveller. You will see vast panoramas like scenes in a Western movie, with dry *playas*, great lakes that have evaporated into salt bowls, and distant, towering mountain ranges shrouded in desert haze. The rocky soil, reddish in color, is punctuated by spectacular rock formations shaped by the wind, and bristles with scrub bush, spiny cacti, yuccas and agaves. You may also spot prickly pears, tarbush and the honey mesquite, which grows around the playas. Plants have to be tough survivors, like the creosote bush, which can survive for two years without any water, by shedding its leaves and branches. You may spot graceful golden eagles cruising the air currents looking for prey such as desert cottontails or black-tailed jack rabbits. On the ground, there are mammals including gray foxes, coyotes and skunks, along with reptiles that include deadly rattlesnakes, the venomous Gila monster and horned lizards that dig holes in the ground to evade the hot desert sun. In summer, an unrelenting, diamond-hard sunlight parches the ground, and the temperature can reach a scorching 109 degrees Fahrenheit (43 degrees Celsius). Come prepared with loose cotton cover-up clothes, a wide-brimmed hat and sun shades, and don't forget to travel with a canteen of water on board. You can explore the desert by following the many hiking and bicycle trails, or try an adventure sport like climbing or caving. The desert is also a photographer's and painter's paradise, and offers many other kinds of activity including *rock hounding* – searching for interesting rocks and gemstones.

GRAMMAR, PUNCTUATION & SPELLING

1. Changing voices

What to do

- Write on the board:
  - Zero took the sneakers.
  - The sneakers were taken by Zero.

- Underline the active and passive verbs. Ask how the verb affects the emphasis of the sentence. (The active verb puts the focus on Zero, the passive on the sneakers.)

- Expand each sentence:
  - Zero took the sneakers. The sneakers had belonged to Clyde Livingston.
  - The sneakers were taken by Zero from a homeless shelter. The shelter was going to auction them to raise money for charity.

- Point out how the object becomes the subject in the sentences that follow on (the shelter and the sneakers). Explain that passive verbs can be used to introduce someone or something that becomes the subject of the next sentence.

- Write: 'Kate Barlow owned the lipstick case.' Ask children to suggest the next sentence, turning the lipstick case into the subject (for example, 'Kate Barlow once owned the lipstick case. It had the initials KB inscribed on it.').

- Challenge pairs to write two sentences about 'Sam', 'Trout Walker', 'The Lake', 'The *Mary Lou*' and 'God's Thumb', following the same pattern.

- Ask volunteers to write their sentences on the board, underlining the objects and subjects.

2. Like this or like that?

What to do

- Work through the interactive activity 'Swap and switch' together, finding suitable synonyms and antonyms. Use the activity to revise the meaning of 'synonyms' and 'antonyms'.

- Read together the opening lines of Chapter 4, describing Stanley's first impressions when he arrives, as far as: 'There weren't even weeds.' Ask the children to pick out adjectives and write them on the board ('dry', 'hard', 'barren', 'desolate', 'run-down'). Revise the meaning of 'synonyms' and 'antonyms' using the adjective 'desolate' (bare, bleak, dreary, and so on).

- Ask pairs to find one or more synonym and antonym for each of the words on the board.

- As a class, work through their suggestions, making lists under each adjective of all the synonyms and antonyms they have found.

- Challenge the pairs to find more descriptive words and phrases about the barren desert landscape in the novel. They should write down phrases and then try to find synonyms and antonyms for as many of the adjectives as they can. Share their findings.

GRAMMAR, PUNCTUATION & SPELLING

3. One word, two meanings

Objective

To distinguish between and use homophones.

What you need

Copies of *Holes*, photocopiable page 22 'Same sounds'.

What to do

- Write the word HOLE on the board in capital letters. Ask the children if they can think of another word that sounds the same but has a different meaning. (whole) Challenge them to use each word in a short sentence about the novel (for example, 'Stanley has to dig a hole every day.'; 'Stanley works hard the whole time he is at camp.').

- Write some more examples of homophones on the board (bare, bear; taut, taught, and so on). Ask volunteers to use each homophone in a sentence to bring out its meaning. Extend the challenge by asking them to think up a sentence that uses both homophones (for example, 'The bear had lost its fur and its coat was looking bare.').

- Hand out the photocopiable page 22 'Same sounds' and ask the children to work in pairs to think of a homophone for the missing words in each sentence.

- Bring the class back together to review their sentences.

Differentiation

Support: Provide one answer for each pair of sentences on the photocopiable sheet and challenge children to find its homophone.
Extension: Challenge pairs of children to construct more sentences about characters or topics from the novel using homophones.

4. Perfect pronouns

Objective

To use relative clauses.
To use commas to clarify meaning.

What you need

Copies of *Holes*, photocopiable page 23 'Additions'.

What to do

- Choose a character or topic from the novel (for example, Sploosh). Ask volunteers to think up a factual statement about the person or topic (for example, 'Sploosh was made from spiced peaches.').

- As a class, think how the statement could be extended using a relative pronoun: who, which, when, and so on (for example, 'Sploosh, which Kate Barlow bottled every summer, was made from spiced peaches.').

- Now, challenge the children to use another pronoun to extend the sentence further (for example, 'Sploosh, which Kate Barlow, who was a teacher at Green Lake, bottled every summer, was made from spiced peaches.').

- Write the sentences on the board, asking the children where to insert commas to help convey meaning and sense.

- Hand out the photocopiable page 23 'Additions' and ask the children to work in pairs to fill it in. Remind them to use punctuation to help divide up their long sentences.

Differentiation

Support: Provide relevant facts to help the children extend the sentences on the photocopiable sheet. Alternatively, work through the page as a shared activity, writing suggestions on the board.
Extension: Children can work in pairs, writing more short factual statements about characters or topics in the novel and challenging their writing partner to use relative pronouns to extend them.

5. Strong words

Objective

To use synonyms.
To use passive verbs.
To use a thesaurus.

What you need

Copies of *Holes*, thesauruses.

What to do

- Write on the board sentences from the novel that describe digging (for example, 'He slammed his shovel into the ground and pried up another piece of earth.' – Chapter 11). Ask the children to identify the verbs ('slammed', 'pried').

- Ask: *Which simpler verb that could replace both?* (dug) Highlight the author's use of synonyms to vary vocabulary and keep the language fresh.

- Ask if these are active or passive verbs (active). Ask: *How do they suit the action they are describing?* (They are strong, active verbs, used to describe the hard, physical action of digging.) Challenge pairs to find other active and passive verbs from the novel or suggest their own, using a thesaurus to help them. Write their suggestions on the board. Invite them to suggest other verbs for digging which have a gentler connotation, again consulting a thesaurus (for example, slid, eased).

- Using the list on the board, ask volunteers for short sentences that use them as passive verbs, and discuss how this alters their impact. 'He slammed his blade into the ground', conveys physical effort more effectively than, 'His blade was slammed into the ground.'

Differentiation

Support: Limit the focus to finding synonyms, and provide chapter or page references to help the children.
Extension: Challenge children to find synonyms for words used to describe other repetitive elements, such as the barren landscape or heat.

6. Speaking the language

Objective

To understand that the spelling of some words needs to be learned specifically.
To use a dictionary.

What you need

Copies of *Holes*, photocopiable page 24 'American English'.

Cross-curricular link

Geography

What to do

- Focus on the setting of the novel. Ask: *Where is the story set?* (America, specifically the Texan desert) *What contributes to the sense of place?* (the landscape, characters/job titles such as the Sheriff and Attorney General, and the language)

- Divide the class into groups. Ask the children to skim and scan the novel, finding words or phrases to compile a glossary of American English. Their nominated note-takers should list words and write the British English 'translation' (for example: 'restroom' = toilet; 'sneakers' = trainers, 'gotten' = got).

- Review the word lists together. Check understanding by inviting volunteers to use words in sentences.

- Hand out the photocopiable page 24 'American English' for the children to fill in.

- Review their work. Highlight key differences in spelling patterns between American and British English (for example, the 'er' (rather than 're') ending of 'theater' and 'center'; the 'se' (rather than 'ce') ending of 'license' (noun) and 'offense'; and the 'or' (rather than 'our') spelling of 'color' and 'odor').

Differentiation

Support: Allow dictionaries or a thesaurus to help them find and spell unfamiliar words.
Extension: Children can extend their glossary using their own knowledge and drawing examples from films, song lyrics and so on.

Same sounds

● For each pair of sentences, think of a word and its homophone to fill the gaps.

1. Stanley is bullied at school about his _____.

   Stanley has a long _____ to be found innocent.

2. Stanley feels he cannot _____ Zero and leave him to die.

   Sploosh would make a tasty _____.

3. Clyde Livingston is known as 'Sweet _____'.

   It is a brave _____ to carry Zero up the mountain.

4. Magnet tells him his first _____ will be the hardest.

   The boys have to dig a hole a day the _____ time they are at Camp Green Lake.

5. When Zero sees it, Stanley hides his letter in the _____ box.

   The water truck wasn't moving – it was _____ on the dirt track.

6. Stanley drives the truck but he fails to use the _____ in time and crashes.

   The boys have short _____ for a drink while they are digging.

Additions

● Extend the following statements using relative pronouns (who, when, which).
Remember to use commas to divide clauses. For example:

> *Green Lake, which is now a dry wasteland, was the largest lake in Texas.*

1. Peach trees once bloomed in Green Lake.

   _____

2. Clyde Livingston was a famous baseball player.

   _____

3. Kate Barlow had robbed Stanley's great-grandfather.

   _____

4. The lipstick case bore the initials KB.

   _____

5. Zero was Madame Zeroni's grandson.

   _____

6. Trout Walker was the son of the richest man in the county.

   _____

American English

● Write the British English words for these American words.

sidewalk		Fall	
pants		diaper	
elevator		trash	

● Write the correct British English spelling for these nouns.

center		license	
color		offense	
theater		traveler	

● Write the British English versions of these expressions and explain what they mean.

British English version	Meaning
two cents' worth	
knock on wood	

1. A new boy

Objective

To describe characters.

What you need

Copies of *Holes*, photocopiable page 29 'A new boy in camp'.

Cross-curricular link

PSHE

What to do

- As a class, find adjectives that describe character or personality and write them on the board (kind, brave, cruel, sensible, lazy, deceitful, naive, helpful, tactful, strong, and so on).

- Divide the class into small groups. Tell each group to choose a character from the story, from the past or present, and decide on three adjectives that best describe them. They can use the list or think up their own. They should support each choice by citing evidence from the story (for example, Stanley is kind because he helps Zero learn to read; he is naive because he thinks the sneakers have just fallen out of the sky).

- Review the devices the author uses to create the boys' characters: physical description (race, colour of hair, glasses, height); habits (Stanley shrugging one shoulder); behaviour (Squid crying at night) and actions (Magnet stealing the sunflower seeds).

- Tell the children they are going to invent a new character who might join Group D. Hand out photocopiable page 29 'A new boy in camp' and ask them to complete it.

- Invite volunteers to introduce their new boy, asking the class to judge which they think would make the most convincing new character and why.

Differentiation

Support: Children can work in their groups to invent a new boy.
Extension: Children can develop their new character by drafting a short piece of description or dialogue featuring them.

2. Map it out

Objective

To describe settings.

What you need

Copies of *Holes*, writing and/or drawing materials.

Cross-curricular link

Geography

What to do

- Tell the children they are going to draw and label a map of Camp Green Lake for use by a new boy, using information found in the novel.

- Arrange them in small groups and ask them to start by scanning the first few chapters of the novel for any information about the camp, such as its layout, any buildings or structures, its location, and so on.

- Provide groups with paper and drawing materials and encourage them to work together to draw their map and label it with key features. They should provide as much information as possible (for example, where the new boy will eat, where he will find his cot or bed, the recreation or 'Wreck Room', and so on).

- When they have finished, invite groups to present their maps and compare and contrast maps by different groups. Ask: *Which is most accurate/easily understood/best presented and why? Do the maps enhance our appreciation of the novel and if so how?* Encourage feedback. Allow groups time to refine and improve their maps and display the most successful.

Differentiation

Support: Provide chapter or page references to find information or work through the information, making notes on the board before the children begin work on their maps.
Extension: Children could use computing skills to construct an alternative image of the camp using the map – for example, a 3D image.

3. Green Lake – past and present

Objective

To describe settings and atmosphere.
To ask questions to improve understanding.

What you need

Copies of *Holes*, photocopiable page 30 'Green Lake: past and present'.

Cross-curricular links

Geography, history

What to do

- Begin by challenging the children to think of some ways their own environment may have changed in the last century. Write some ideas on the board (for example, cars, aeroplanes, clothes).

- Ask the children to suggest any causes or triggers for these changes (new inventions or discoveries; the two World Wars, which speeded up change, and so on).

- Explain to the children that they are now going to think about the contrasts between Green Lake as it was 110 years ago, and as it is when Stanley is there. Invite them to cite some of the differences (climate and weather, plants and landscape, population).

- Ask: *What do you think has brought about the dramatic changes at Green Lake?* (Global warming? A curse brought on by a cruel racist murder?)

- Hand out photocopiable page 30 'Green Lake: past and present' and allow children time to complete it, working in pairs.

Differentiation

Support: Challenge children to use the information on their completed sheets to draw and label maps of Green Lake then and now.
Extension: Challenge children to write a short diary entry or speech by someone who is old enough to remember Green Lake as it was, who is shocked when they return to find how it has changed.

4. The Texan desert

Objective

To select the appropriate form for the purpose of writing.

What you need

Copies of *Holes*, media resources 'Texan desert', 'Wind-eroded rock', and 'Texan desert writing frame'.

Cross-curricular link

Geography, computing

What to do

- Explain that this lesson will focus on the setting for *Holes*: the Texan desert. The children will gather information on the desert, looking at key features such as terrain, climate and wildlife.

- Discuss words describing the desert – focus on landscape, plants, and weather. Display the photograph of the desert as a visual stimulus.

- Display the photograph of the rock and use it to trigger discussion of desert canyons and rocks. Ask if they know how desert rocks like God's Thumb get their shape. (They are carved over time by erosion: the wind blows sand against them, gradually wearing parts away.)

- Which desert creatures can the children recall from the story? (yellow-spotted lizards, rattlesnakes, scorpions, tarantulas)

- Explain that the children are going to plan a non-chronological report on the Texan desert, gathering all the evidence they can from the novel. Revise key features of the genre, such as general opening and concluding statements, factual objective style.

- Allow time for pairs to fill in the writing frame.

Differentiation

Support: Find relevant information together before the children attempt the writing frame.
Extension: Children can draft a report on the Texan desert using information gathered. They can use computing skills to complete this task.

5. Destiny's work

Objective

To draw inferences, justifying with evidence.
To ask questions to improve understanding.

What you need

Copies of *Holes*, photocopiable page 31 'Superstitions'.

Cross-curricular link

RE

What to do

- Tell the children that this lesson will focus on the idea of destiny or fate. They will consider how destiny seems to shape Stanley's fortune, interweaving his life with that of earlier generations of his family. They will focus on the idea of superstitions, such as the gypsy's curse, and the idea of Green Lake being punished by a drought for the racist murder there.

- Read from the middle of Chapter 6, 'On the day Stanley was arrested…', to the end of the chapter. Ask why Stanley feels that these sneakers are special. (They seem like a sign or a gift from God.)

- Focus on the phrase 'destiny's shoes'. Challenge children to explain what this means. Ask: *Can you identify other words that reflect the same concept?* ('…some kind of sign', 'seemingly out of nowhere', 'like a gift from God')

- As a class, consider how the sneakers determine Stanley's destiny and affect other characters' lives.

- Give each child photocopiable page 31 'Superstitions'. Encourage them to consider how specific elements from the novel demonstrate the presence of superstitious belief in the story.

Differentiation

Support: Prepare by discussing the concept of superstitious beliefs, citing familiar examples.
Extension: Challenge the children to discuss their views on the moral basis of the story. Ask: *What seems fair and what seems unfair? Do things come right and if so how and why?*

6. Looking ahead

Objective

To infer characters' feelings.
To predict what might happen.

What you need

Copies of *Holes*.

Cross-curricular links

PSHE, citizenship, computing

What to do

- Re-read Chapter 12. Ask a child to summarise the purpose of Mr Pedanski's meeting with the boys (to discuss their future paths and ambitions). Ask: *Why would this be important for the boys at the camp?* (To give them motivation and help them think about getting their lives back on track.)

- Ask: *What becomes of Zero at the end?* (He is reunited with his mother, friendly with Stanley's family and with Clyde Livingston.) *What sort of work might he go on to do?* Encourage children to speculate and support their answers with reasons. (for example, he might become an accountant as he is good at mathematics) Repeat the exercise focusing on Stanley. Ask: *What might he do?* (Teach? Be an inventor like his father? Become a detective?)

- Ask groups to choose one of the other characters and speculate on what he might do when he leaves camp. Share ideas, encouraging evidence from the novel.

Differentiation

Support: Provide groups with questions to help them predict and speculate about a character: *What is his real name? Why was he at camp? What is he good at? What words or actions tell us something about his character?*
Extension: Children could use computing skills to draft a CV for their chosen character, fleshing out details such as why he was at camp and what he goes on to do when he leaves.

7. Looking back

Objective

To ask questions to improve understanding.
To identify how structure contributes to meaning.
To make comparisons within books.

What you need

Copies of *Holes*, interactive activity 'Flashbacks'.

What to do

- Tell the children they are going to investigate how the author uses flashbacks to make the experience of reading the story more interesting, with events in the present echoing or being somehow linked with those from the past.

- Point out that the chronological order of events (the order in which they happen) differs from the order in which they appear in the novel – the narrative jumps backwards and forwards as events are revealed. Challenge volunteers to cite chapters or points in the novel where this happens.

- Display the interactive activity 'Flashbacks', and work through it together as a shared activity.

- Next, the children should attempt the activity in pairs – this time, rearranging events in the order in which they appear in the narrative.

- As a class, compare and contrast the narrative order with the chronological order and discuss how the author interweaves past and present, and what this contributes to the novel (a sense of changing times; the legacy of past wrongs or grievances, and so on).

Differentiation

Support: Provide, or work through together, a bulleted list of key events in the past and present to support the tasks.
Extension: The children could experiment by altering the order of episodes to see what impact it might have on developing the narrative.

8. Style and effect

Objective

To identify how language, structure and presentation contribute to meaning.
To learn technical terms such as simile, imagery, style and effect.

What you need

Copies of *Holes*, interactive activity 'Style and content'.

What to do

- Tell the children that they are going to reflect on the style and tone of writing that the author uses, and how it suits the narrative and plot.

- List on the board a range of style and language features such as: 'formal, informal and descriptive language', 'poetry', 'imagery', 'simile and metaphor', 'repetition', 'synonyms'.

- Arrange the children into small groups and ask each to skim and scan the novel to find one or more examples of the listed features.

- Display the interactive activity 'Style and content'. Explain to the children that the task is to try to match each style feature with its purpose or effect. Demonstrate this by modelling the first answer:
  Feature: Simple, sparse prose style
  Purpose/effect: Creates sense of bleak desert landscape and harsh camp conditions.

Differentiation

Support: Work through the interactive activity as a shared task.
Extension: Challenge children to work in pairs to extend the interactive activity by adding more features and effects.

A new boy in camp

- Invent a new boy character who has just arrived at the camp.

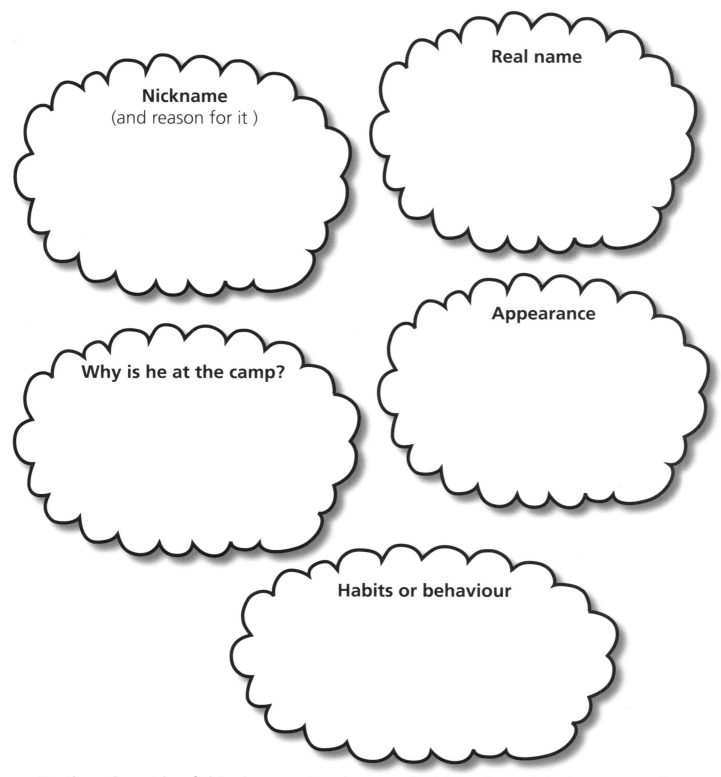

Nickname
(and reason for it)

Real name

Why is he at the camp?

Appearance

Habits or behaviour

- On the other side of this sheet, write about an incident that might happen at Camp Green Lake that shows his character.

Green Lake: past and present

● Compare Green Lake as it was 110 years ago and as it is now.

Then	Now
●	●
●	●
●	●
●	●

● Write some quotes by the characters who remember the lake as it used to be.

Sam

Doc Hawthorn

Miss Katherine

Superstitions

● Make notes on how the following subjects demonstrate superstitious belief in the story.

a gypsy's curse

a pair of sneakers

onions

a drought

● Write about another superstition from the story on the other side of this sheet.

TALK ABOUT IT

1. The whole truth

Objective
To give well-structured descriptions, explanations and narratives.

What you need
Copies of *Holes*, media resource 'Chain reaction'.

What to do
- Tell the children that they are going to focus on the events that lead to Stanley's arrest. They will gather evidence to construct an accurate verbal recount of what really happened.

- Read from the middle of Chapter 6, 'On the day Stanley was arrested…', to the end of the chapter. Encourage children to extract the key sequence of events.

- Display the media resource 'Chain reaction' and fill the writing frame in together, arranging events in chronological order. Ask the children to recall what happened, referring to Chapter 41 for evidence if necessary. Ask: *What are the names of the key characters involved in the episode?* (Stanley, Derrick, Zero, the police officer, the driver of the car)

- Ask: *What began the chain of events?* (Zero stole the sneakers from the shelter.) *What put Stanley in the frame?* (He was walking home because he had missed the bus.)

- Arrange the children in small groups. Tell them to work together on a verbal recount of the chain of events. Invite volunteers from groups to present their recount. Encourage feedback on which recounts are most concise and comprehensive.

Differentiation
Support: Provide key page references and tell each group to appoint a note-taker who will record facts they can use for their recount.
Extension: Groups can draft their recount. Encourage them to use appropriate temporal or causal connectives, such as 'then', 'after' and 'because'.

2. Right or wrong?

Objective
To draw inferences, justifying them with evidence. To participate in performances, role play, improvisations and debates.

What you need
Copies of *Holes*, photocopiable page 35 'Crime scenes'.

Cross-curricular links
Citizenship, drama

What to do
- Re-read Chapter 6. Arrange the children in groups to plan and rehearse a short drama on the trial. Roles can include: Stanley, the policeman who arrested him, a prosecuting lawyer, the judge, a representative of the homeless shelter, an eyewitness, Clyde Livingston and Stanley's parents. Provide the photocopiable page 35 'Crime scenes' as prompts for dialogue.

- Allow time to rehearse; then invite the groups to perform. When they have finished, discuss how the trial went and why Stanley was not able to convince the judge of his innocence. Ask: *Why does Stanley not declare his innocence, even at camp? What makes him endure his fate until he is found innocent?* (stoicism or lack of confidence?) Elicit the reasons he might go along with his 'destiny'. (He believes he is under a family curse; he does not understand where the sneakers came from.)

- Discuss how this apparent misfortune has positive outcomes for Stanley and for Green Lake. (He makes a new best friend; he finds his great-grandfather's suitcase; he rights a wrong from the past, lifting the family curse, as well as the drought.)

Differentiation
Support: Help children plan a structure for dialogue for their drama scene.
Extension: Encourage children to discuss other ways the novel deals with moral issues; for example, the killing of an innocent man for racist motives.

3. Natural revenge

Objective

To infer characters' feelings.
To participate in performances, role play, improvisations and debates.
To use spoken language to develop understanding through imagining and exploring ideas.

What you need

Copies of *Holes*.

Cross-curricular links

Citizenship, drama, music

What to do

- Divide the class into groups to prepare short dramas about the drought that strikes Green Lake after the racist killing of Sam.

- The children should imagine they are a group of locals discussing what has happened and what they think has caused it. Roles could include a farmer whose crops are dying for lack of rain and someone who can no longer swim in the lake. They should refer to the novel for evidence (for example, the peach trees are dying, the lake dries up and it becomes a desert landscape).

- Suggest that the characters might express different views – some might not believe superstition; others might believe it is punishment from God. Allow the groups sufficient time to plan and perform their scenes. Walk around and observe them as they practise.

- Invite groups to perform their dramas for the class. Encourage feedback and constructive criticism.

Differentiation

Support: Provide groups with a list of roles and character notes: for example, a farmer whose crops have died because of drought.
Extension: Learners can follow up their drama by planning and writing a scene from a play about the drought, using dialogue from some of the characters they played.

4. Camp Fun and Games

Objective

To consider and evaluate different viewpoints, attending to and building on the contributions of others.

What you need

Copies of *Holes*, media resource 'Rules in camp'.

Cross-curricular links

PSHE, citizenship

What to do

- Together, scan Chapters 4 to 10 and summarise Stanley's daily routine at the camp.

- Discuss how Stanley imagines the camp before he goes ('Camp Fun and Games') and how it really is (a harsh juvenile reform camp). Explain that orange (the colour of the boys' clothes) is used for prison clothes in the United States.

- Display the media resource 'Rules in camp'. Tell the children they are going to draft a list of Camp Green Lake rules to hand to new boys. Complete the writing frame together.

- Introduce the terms 'holiday camp', 'boot camp' and 'brat camp'. Encourage dialogue about their aims and methods. Discuss that brat camps try to turn around youngsters with behavioural problems. Identify features Camp Green Lake shares with boot/brat camps (strict discipline, physical challenges, outdoor exercise).

- Invite views: *Are brat camps a good idea? Do you think they work? Does Stanley get any benefits from his stay?* (He gets physically fit, makes a good friend, learns about himself and does some growing up.)

Differentiation

Support: Provide key headings to focus ideas for the writing frame: 'clothes', 'meals', 'water', 'work', 'punishments,' 'rewards'.
Extension: Challenge children to design a web page about Camp Green Lake, using persuasive language to promote it as a juvenile reform camp.

5. Desert dangers

Objective

To identify and discuss themes.
To gain, maintain and monitor the interest of the listener(s).
To select and use appropriate registers for effective communication.

What you need

Copies of *Holes*, photocopiable page 36 'Desert survival'.

Cross-curricular links

Geography, science

What to do

- Tell the children that this lesson will focus on the risks and dangers the boys face at Camp Green Lake. Challenge them to list some of the dangers (sunburn, lizard bites, and so on) and write them on the board.

- Hand out photocopiable page 36 'Desert survival' and allow time for pairs to complete it.

- When they have finished, ask the children to rate the dangers in order of severity and support their choices with evidence. Ask: *Which dangers might cause pain or discomfort? Which might be deadly?*

- Arrange the children in groups to prepare a short talk on the dangers the boys face, to help prepare new boys for the risks. They should offer advice on how best to avoid or deal with each danger. Allow groups time to prepare their talk, and nominate a speaker.

- Invite speakers from each group to give their talk and discuss how effective it would be, and how it could be improved.

Differentiation

Support: Review the ideas on the photocopiable sheet together, discussing how best boys at the camp can avoid each danger.
Extension: Children can use computing skills to make a short video presentation or podcast that would be helpful for new boys.

6. I shot the sheriff!

Objective

To infer characters' feelings, thoughts and motives.
To participate in performances, role play and improvisations.

What you need

Copies of *Holes*, photocopiable page 37 'Interview notes'.

Cross-curricular links

Citizenship, drama, computing

What to do

- Divide the class into groups to prepare and act out a short television report about Kate Barlow's shooting of the Sheriff at Green Lake. One child plays the part of the reporter, and others play locals such as Trout Walker (see Chapter 23), Dr Hawthorn and Hattie Parker (see Chapter 25). Remind children to think about the bias each person might have regarding Kate and her romance with Sam.

- Using the photocopiable page 37 'Interview notes' as a prompt sheet, encourage children to think about questions the reporter would ask, using the formula 'who, what, when, where, why?' *What had led to the shooting? Why was Kate so angry with the Sheriff? What did the locals think about her?*

- They should consider the reactions of the locals – some characters might praise Kate's teaching, others might disapprove of her romance with Sam.

- Visit each group and invite groups to perform their report and encourage constructive feedback.

Differentiation

Support: As a class, gather facts about the people interviewed and write them on the board as support for character portrayal.
Extension: Children could try making a video or podcast or plan a newspaper report featuring the interviews with locals.

Crime scenes

- Use the storyboard to help recount the events that led to Stanley's arrest.

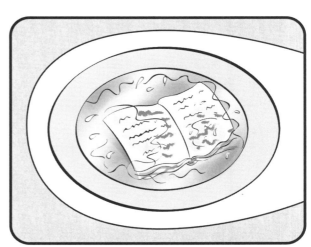

Desert survival

● Look at the pictures below and, next to each one, describe why they pose risks and dangers to the boys at Camp Green Lake.

Interview notes

● Use these prompt notes to help you frame information for your character's speech.

Reporters ask the five 'W' questions to get key information: who, what, when, where, why?
The notes here have been completed for Hattie Parker.

Who? *Hattie Parker*

What? *enraged at seeing the Negro onion seller Sam kissing the schoolteacher Katherine Barlow*

When? *on a rainy day at the end of the first school semester*

Where? *outside the schoolhouse, as she stepped from the general store*

Why? *because she believes it is a sin against God for a Negro man and white woman to kiss*

Notes on character:
● Use this box to write notes on your character, fleshing out with more detail from your imagination.

> *Hattie Parker – lives alone; single; has always lived at Green Lake; keeps herself and her house very spick and span; is the neighbourhood gossip; has old-fashioned and racist views.*

▼ GET WRITING

1. Deadly critters

Objective

To ask questions to improve understanding. To assess the effectiveness of their own and others' writing and suggest improvements.

What you need

Copies of *Holes*, media resource 'Mexican beaded lizard', photocopiable page 41 'Desert wildlife guide'.

Cross-curricular links

Geography, science, computing

What to do

- Ask the children to recall the deadly creatures Stanley encounters at Camp Green Lake (rattlesnakes, yellow-spotted lizards). Display the image of the lizard and explain that the author invented a deadly lizard based on venomous lizards such as the Mexican beaded lizard.

- Re-read Chapter 8, telling the children to scan for facts about the lizards in preparation for planning a report on them. Hand out photocopiable page 41 and ask the children to work in pairs to fill it in.

- Organise the children in groups and set them the challenge of inventing another deadly creature that Stanley might encounter. It could be another type of lizard or snake, or something different, but it should be convincing as a desert animal.

- Allow them time to discuss and invent their animal, and then fill in another copy of the photocopiable page using their ideas.

- Invite volunteers to describe their animal to the class, and discuss which sound most convincing, and which would be most scary or deadly.

Differentiation

Support: Limit the work on their own invention to group discussion, and presentation of their ideas to their classmates.
Extension: Children could use computing skills to develop their report on yellow-spotted lizards for a desert wildlife guide.

2. A letter home

Objective

To identify audience and purpose of writing and select the appropriate form.

What you need

Copies of *Holes*, printable page 'Writing home'.

What to do

- Remind the children of the letter that Stanley begins writing home to his parents. Re-read the relevant part of Chapter 18.

- Ask them why they think Stanley fibs in his letter (to save his parents worry and upset). Ask: *What does this tell us about his character?* (He is caring; he loves his parents; he is grown up enough to deal with the hardship on his own; he shows bravery, stoicism and stamina.)

- Hand out printable page 'Writing home' and ask the children to work in pairs to finish off Stanley's letter in the same tone. Ask: *What might he go on to say about the other boys? What might he say about the staff at the camp?*

- When they have finished, set children the task of writing another letter, this time telling Stanley's parents the truth.

- Discuss the letters, and which one they think it is best for Stanley to send and why. Ask: *How do they think his parents would react to each letter?*

Differentiation

Support: Before children begin, as a class, list on the board ideas for content Stanley might include in each letter on the board.
Extension: Challenge the children to write replies from Stanley's mother to each version of Stanley's letter home.

3. Stanley's diary

Objective

To infer characters' feelings.
To select appropriate form for purpose of writing.
To distinguish between formal and informal language.

What you need

Copies of *Holes*, photocopiable page 42 'Stanley's diary'.

Cross-curricular links

PSHE, citizenship

What to do

- Explain to the children that they are going to recount events that happen to Stanley in the form of a diary he might keep. Briefly review key features of diary writing (first person, past tense, may be informal writing; may include reflective/subjective emotions). Ask the children whether they can think of any famous books that are written in diary form (for example, *The Diary of a Young Girl* by Anne Frank, *The Diary of a Killer Cat* by Anne Fine and *The Secret Diary of Adrian Mole Aged 13¾* by Sue Townsend).

- Give out photocopiable page 42 'Stanley's diary'. Explain that the children should write an entry for either Stanley's first day at camp or for the day he visits the warden.

- Remind them they should include Stanley's emotions and feelings (for example, they should consider how he felt when Derrick put his notebook in the toilet and also when the police patrol car pulled up).

Differentiation

Support: Provide some question prompts when they are writing their diary entries. For example, ask: *What are the main events that happen? How do they make Stanley feel?*
Extension: The children can write another entry describing a significant day; for example, the day that Stanley gets arrested or the day he finds the lipstick case.

4. The late Kissin' Kate

Objective

To identify audience and purpose of writing and select the appropriate form.

What you need

Copies of *Holes*, media resource 'Annie Oakley', media resource 'Obituary', examples of print or online obituaries of famous people.

Cross-curricular link

History

What to do

- Re-read Chapter 13 up to the initials 'KB'. Ask: *What is the mystery object that Stanley has found? What can you remember about Kate Barlow? Who was she? What did she do? How did she die?*

- Watch the video clip of Annie Oakley. There is no commentary for this clip. Explain that she was a famous performing 'sharpshooter' in the 19th century. Along with real-life female outlaws, such as Belle Starr and Pearl Hart, she inspired films that were popular in the 1940s.

- Display the media resource 'Obituary' and insert headings, such as 'Appearance', 'Character', 'Job,' 'Famous for' and 'Events'. Tell the children that they are going to plan an obituary for Kissin' Kate that might appear in a local newspaper. If possible, refer to examples of obituaries of famous people.

- Fill in the writing frame together, inviting children to volunteer facts about Kate. (She made spiced peaches, she was a teacher at the school, and so on – see Chapter 23.) Discuss how to shape the material into a concise obituary. Ask: *Which are the most important facts and how would you organise them?*

Differentiation

Support: Scan Chapter 3 as a class activity for facts to record on the writing frame.
Extension: Children could draft an obituary about Kate for the local newspaper.

5. A better way

Objective

To discuss themes.
To organise paragraphs around a theme.

What you need

Copies of *Holes*, photocopiable page 43 'Bulldog Kids' Camp'.

Cross-curricular links

PSHE, citizenship, computing

What to do

- Tell the children that they are going to discuss ideas for a genuine juvenile 'reform' camp, to improve behaviour in children who have done wrong or committed a crime.

- Display photocopiable page 43 'Bulldog Kids' Camp'.

- Arrange the children into small groups. Tell them that they should spend some time discussing what they think would work best to improve behaviour in children who need to turn their lives around.

- They should first think about the purposes of their camp – to motivate, inspire, build character, encourage teamwork, and so on. They should go on to discuss activities that might foster this, which could include sports, team games, or boot-camp style trials or assault courses. Encourage them to consider other aspects, such as whether they would have a uniform, the staff, and so on.

- Hand out the photocopiable sheets and allow groups time to fill them in. Invite a volunteer from each group to present their plan to the class.

- Encourage feedback on which camps the children think would work best, and why.

Differentiation

Support: Provide examples of activities at boot and brat camps to get children started.
Extension: Let groups use computing skills to turn the ideas on their writing frame into a leaflet or brochure to promote the camp to parents and other interested parties.

6. The wonderful onion

Objective

To use organisational and presentational features to structure text.
To distinguish between statements of fact and opinion.

What you need

Copies of *Holes*.

Cross-curricular links

Art and design, science, computing

What to do

- Divide the class into small groups and tell them they are going to design an advertisement for Sam's onion cures. They should refer to Chapters 25 and 40 to find information such as what he claimed to cure, the different ointments and lotions he made.

- Before they begin, discuss whether they think onions genuinely have healing powers. (Scientists regard them as a 'super food', high in vitamin C and other important nutrients; they can act as a powerful antibiotic and also help maintain healthy blood pressure.) If there is time, they could use computing skills to research facts on the internet.

- Check that the children understand the concepts of slogans and logos by referring to familiar brands. Revise persuasive features of advertisements – a catchy slogan, humour, emotive language and so on.

- Groups should nominate a note-taker and then work together to plan their advertisement. They should think of a slogan and decide how the advert should be worded and illustrated.

- Ask volunteers from each group to present their ideas. Invite constructive feedback, considering the persuasive features: Vote for the best advertisement.

Differentiation

Support: Scan Chapters 25 and 40 as a class activity to find relevant facts.
Extension: Children can use computing skills to develop their advertisements.

Desert wildlife guide

● Discuss and invent another deadly creature. Fill in the details about the animal below.

DEADLY CREATURES ■

Name of animal/species

_____

Appearance/markings

_____

_____

Habitat

_____

Diet/prey

_____

Behaviour

_____

_____

_____

☠ Secret weapon

_____

_____

_____

6

WILDLIFE GUIDE

Stanley's diary

● Fill in this diary. The second entry should be about Stanley's first day at camp or his visit to the Warden.

The day I got arrested _____

The day... _____

Useful words: ratio, notebook, sneakers, overpass, orange clothes, cold shower, smelly cot, venom, screams, nail polish, make-up case

Bulldog Kids' Camp

- Talk about how you could help children to improve their behaviour.
- Plan your ideas for Bulldog Kids' Camp below.

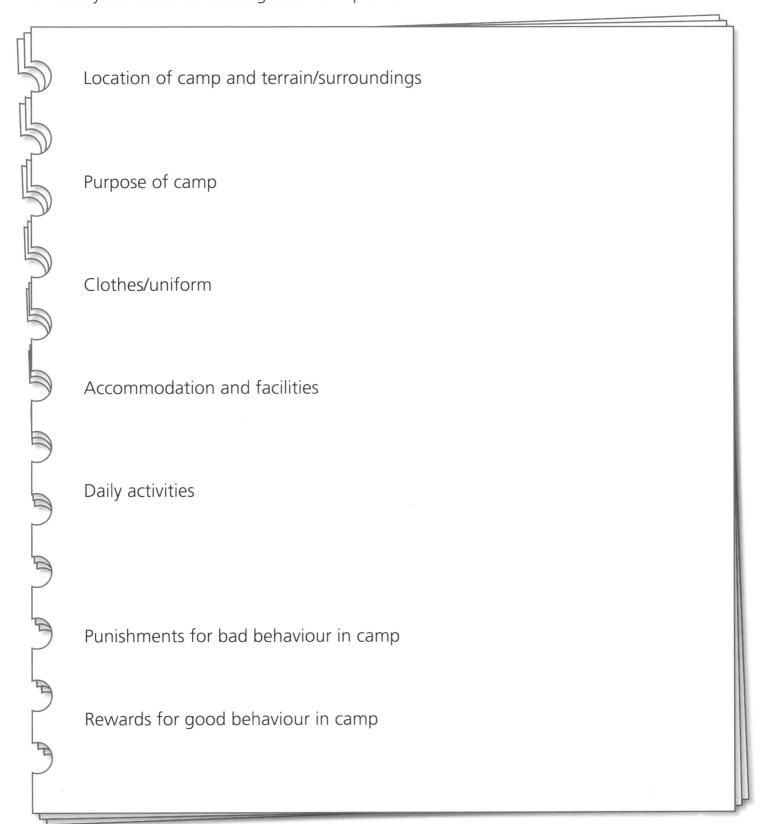

Location of camp and terrain/surroundings

Purpose of camp

Clothes/uniform

Accommodation and facilities

Daily activities

Punishments for bad behaviour in camp

Rewards for good behaviour in camp

▼ ASSESSMENT

1. Nameless

Objective

To précis longer passages.
To summarise the main ideas drawn from more than one paragraph.

What you need

Copies of *Holes*.

What to do

- Write on the board the titles of the three parts of the novel. Discuss the titles, and how they act as 'hooks' for the reader; for example, the first part is introduced by a title that mimics a road sign, and tells us we are going to enter a place called Camp Green Lake.

- Point out that the author has only used chapter numbers, not titles. Tell the children they are going to skim and scan the chapters and think of titles for them. The titles should give an idea of the content of the chapter without giving away too much of the plot, and act as a hook to make the reader want to read on.

- Discuss some ideas for chapter titles and write them on the board: for example, Chapter 4 might be 'Arrival in camp' or 'First impressions'.

- Arrange the children into small groups and assign them five or six chapters. They should skim and scan the chapters to find a suitable title. Allow them time to think up and list their ideas, then bring the class back together to review their ideas.

Differentiation

Support: Choose six chapters from the novel and skim and scan them together to invent titles.
Extension: Challenge children to think of titles that mimic the style of the author's titles for each part.

2. Big issues

Objective

To identify and discuss themes.

What you need

Copies of *Holes*, photocopiable page 47 'Themes and threads'.

Cross-curricular link

RE

What to do

- Begin by asking the children if they can identify the main themes of the novel.

- Ask them to support their suggestions with reasons (for example, 'I think righting a wrong is a main theme because when Stanley carries Zero up the mountain he is putting right the wrong his great-great-grandfather did when he failed to carry Madame Zeroni up the mountain.', or, 'I think growing up is a main theme because Stanley grows up a lot while he is at camp, and changes from a victim of bullies into a heroic character.').

- Write their suggestions for themes on the board and discuss which, if any, they would identify as the most important theme, again encouraging them to give reasons.

- Hand out photocopiable page 47 'Themes and threads' and ask the children to fill it in, working in pairs or individually.

Differentiation

Support: Work through the photocopiable page as a shared activity, making brief notes on the board before the children begin writing.
Extension: Invite children to explore the main themes further. For example, they might consider the idea of righting a wrong through the Christian concept of 'the sins of the fathers' being visited on the sons, or the Buddhist idea of Karma.

3. Holes: the quiz

Objective

To explain and discuss their understanding of what they have read.
To provide reasoned justifications for their views.

What you need

Copies of *Holes*, interactive activity 'Fill in the holes'.

What to do

- Tell the children they are going to try a multiple-choice quiz about the novel. Let them attempt the interactive activity 'Fill in the holes' working in small groups. They can check their scores when they finish, and compare scores between groups.

- Challenge groups to compile their own quiz questions about the novel. They could attempt another multiple-choice quiz, or write statements for a true-or-false quiz.

- Model some examples on the board:
  - True or false? Trout Walker shoots the Sheriff of Green Lake: answer – false.
  - True or false? Hector Zeroni steals sneakers from a homeless shelter: answer – true.

- Groups can then challenge each other to answer their quiz questions. When they have finished, review scores and announce winning teams or groups.

- Encourage feedback, identifying which quiz questions were most challenging and why.

Differentiation

Support: Model further questions for each type of quiz on the board before groups begin and discuss some quiz questions or statements together.
Extension: Groups can attempt to devise more difficult or challenging quizzes about the novel.

4. Threads

Objective

To recognise and compare themes in what they read.

What you need

Copies of *Holes*.

Cross-curricular link

PSHE

What to do

- Together, read the back cover blurb and reviews about the novel. Ask the children to extract words or phrases indicating important themes in the novel (a mystery and its solution – 'dig up the truth', detective plot, friendship). Write these on the board.

- Ask children to continue listing the other themes (avenging or righting a wrong, growing up, coming of age, and so on). Add these to the list. If the children have recently read any other novels that cover similar themes, invite comparisons, focusing on key features such as plot and style, and encouraging subjective opinion ('I think this is more exciting/unusual/interesting because…').

- Invite children to choose the theme they think is most significant or has most impact on them. They should draft a short statement beginning, 'I think Holes is a novel about…' describing the theme and why it is important (for example, 'I think Holes is a novel about friendship because, although life at camp is hard, Stanley and Hector help each other survive and become best friends.').

- Invite volunteers to read out their statements, and encourage feedback.

Differentiation

Support: Discuss the main themes as a class, using the list on the board as a starting point before the children begin drafting their statements.
Extension: Children can construct mind maps showing main themes in the novel with notes about each.

5. Detective work

Objective

To explain and discuss their understanding of what they have read.
To provide reasoned justifications for their views.

What you need

Copies of *Holes*, brief reviews of the novel.

What to do

- Ask a volunteer to read aloud the *Guardian* newspaper review from the back cover of the novel. Arrange the children in small groups and ask them to discuss the content of the review, and what they think the reviewer means. Ask: *In what ways is the story funny or humorous? In what ways is it 'tightly plotted' and how is it a 'detective novel'? What do you think the reviewer means when he says it is a 'generous' book?*

- Groups should nominate a note-taker who can write down ideas under headings as they discuss. Bring the class back together to review and discuss their findings.

- Challenge groups to draft another short review for the novel, which could appear on the back cover and would encourage readers to want to read the novel. Encourage them to try to identify different aspects of the novel. Invite volunteers to present their review to the class, and encourage feedback.

Differentiation

Support: Before groups begin, share ideas on each aspect of the review and write them on the board under headings: 'Humourous', 'Generous', 'Tightly plotted', 'Detective novel'.

Extension: Groups can prepare a short presentation for the class, explaining and supporting the ideas behind their reviews.

6. Book club

Objective

To explain and discuss their understanding of what they have read.
To provide reasoned justifications for their views.

What you need

Copies of *Holes*.

What to do

- Explain that the children are going to pretend they are appearing on the radio for a book-club programme, reviewing the novel *Holes*.

- Discuss some questions that the programme's presenter might ask, and list them on the board. For example:
  - Did you enjoy the novel and if so why?
  - What is your favourite part of the novel and why?
  - Do you like the main character Stanley?
  - Did you feel the ending was satisfactory?

- Allow them time to work on their own to prepare some notes on what they think or feel about the novel. Encourage them to refer to the novel and to back up their views with evidence. (for example, 'I think Holes is an exciting story because you want to find out the real reason why the boys have to dig every day.')

- Appoint a presenter who will give a brief introduction to the book, and then invite others to participate in a group discussion about the novel. The presenter can use the questions on the board and add more of their own.

Differentiation

Support: Children could work in pairs to discuss their opinions on the novel before they begin the book-club discussion.

Extension: Children could use computing skills to make a podcast or video of the book club.

Themes and threads

- Explain how these themes feature in the novel.

Racial hatred

Paying for past sins or wrongs

Racial harmony

Bullying

Growing up

Friendship

SCHOLASTIC

Available in this series:

978-1407-14220-3

978-1407-14219-7

978-1407-14224-1

978-1407-14222-7

978-1407-14223-4

978-1407-15875-4

978-1407-14225-8

978-1407-15877-8

978-1407-14228-9

978-1407-14231-9

978-1407-14226-5 **MAY 2016**

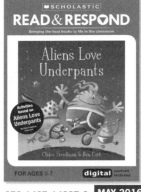

978-1407-14227-2 **MAY 2016**

978-1407-14230-2 **MAY 2016**

978-1407-15876-1 **MAY 2016**

978-1407-15879-2 **MAY 2016**

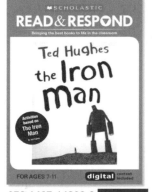

978-1407-14229-6 **MAY 2016**

To find out more, call: 0845 6039091
or visit our website www.scholastic.co.uk/readandrespond